dated emcees

chinaka hodge

city lights books | san francisco

Cover image: Papercut portrait of the author by Miriam Klein Stahl, based on a photograph by Scott LaRockwell

Library of Congress Cataloging-in-Publication Data
Names: Hodge, Chinaka, author.
Title: Dated emcees / Chinaka Hodge.
Description: San Francisco : City Lights Books, [2016]
Identifiers: LCCN 2016005740 | ISBN 9780872867024 (paperback) | ISBN 780872867253 (ebook)
Subjects: LCSH: Hip-hop–Poetry. | BISAC: POETRY / American / African American. | MUSIC / Genres & Styles / Rap & Hip Hop. | POETRY / American /
  General.
Classification: LCC PS3608.O45 A6 2016 | DDC 811/.6–dc23
LC record available at https://lccn.loc.gov/2016005740

City Lights books are published at the City Lights Bookstore
261 Columbus Avenue, San Francisco, CA 94133
www.citylights.com

for sherane
who showed up late to the barbeque and

who was the entire west coast with the oakland ass and the
janet braids and the spare apartment off leimert where it was
safe. whose titties hung low off the mouth of the chicagoan
and then he had the nerve to talk about it on wax who sat on
a faux leather couch wedged crooked in the spare closet of his
cousin's room who pushed tree shavings around a level surface
moved malt liquor bottles to the trash reapplied lipstick cuffed
the bottom of her jeans listened to the same sample over and
over waited for the illegal patches to load damned protools for
failing while the session exported re-twisted her one loose braid
and covered her mouth barricading curses for his head and the
hands that will not touch her like they are invested.

for sherane who died
for the record

dated emcees

on a fall evening in the early aughts old uncle rap
pulls up his gut, inspects the waistband of his track
pants, catches his reflection in a dull passing train,
decides it is time for honors, decrees let us throw a party,
let us invite some children, tell them of the days golden
and silvering our hair, someone, book the venue,
roll the linoleum, rig a streetlight, polish some statues
— and it was done.

bet, so, first fall in the new millennium, i'm invited
to rock for the legends at this party. i'm eighteen,
gangly and in an impromptu cipher of washed up
rappers, finger-dead can holders, uprocking on
inflamed knees, asking what to do with the next decade,
these medallions, felt caps, izods, really, still izods? okay
sure whatever, old dudes rocking old fits in new york on this
the twenty-third day of autumn smoking loosies
and spliffs outside the stage door of symphony space.
you know. high. art.

nobody does today's mathematics, the last night of hip hop
as they know it and they don't even know it, college drop
out ain't dropped yet, auto-tune forthcoming, common
got a record out everyone hates; it's a circus of miserable
electric clowns.

so okay i shit you not the first nword to size me up
appraise me as sex-able if perhaps groupie, knows
i'm too young for his music, probably never heard
of the guy, definitely don't recognize him, is someone

round greying in a shirt that came with the pants
and a pair of gazelles actually older than my father.
he hands me his business card and real talk no need
to shit you as I said before it reads across the front

positive k: rapper.

on coke white mid-grade stock & he like you should
call me sometime & i'm like i don't think i can &
he like why not & since this is probably the only
time i'll be able to land this line, walk this way &
fuck it he'll probably get a kick out of it

he like why not
i'm like
i got a man.

title track

no jazz men left: i date emcees,
tries to rehabilitate them,
into honest, working stiffs
i foot the bills, handle
the losses they come
loud leave softly
fall short break
daylight
gone

say word i got a million of em
a queue of emcees so lettered
credentialed craft me vacant
scalped me naked nearly
took my head and ran
towards the hit
there's the groove
in the heart
crushed cold
game

i confess i love fast dishonest
words, thoughts, childish aliases
men who changed their names, forced rhyme
divulged they governments,
and then forgot mine
the lames i held
on too long
way past
time

time. again. first words penned since the spurn,
scents of sweated-out perms and burns
her panties. my pillowcase
apologies on wax
forgive the tone
so over
under
you

i date lushes faded like grandpops
who crawl sixteen bars and get twisted
they run tabs more than they spit
swallow fake beautifuls
hen and mott's apple
juiced stuck slurs stirs
one finger
skyward
blurred

but if a rapper treated me sweet
i'd break him for shits and snickers
there i said it. truth. uncut.
ugly, buck ass naked
late night video
vixen over
sexed vexed writes
book sells
out

call me karrine steffans. you know, uh
superhead, you know uh, dirty
drawers aired in mixed company
read me. tell all. real talk.
fucked a few maybe
sucked em off good
sycophant
getting
press

real talk i don't even care no more
i hear the speakers age poorly
see their cables get frayed, fade
nothing worse. a washed out
monitor lapsing
squeaking feedback
nothing new
high-pitched
wail

and whose fault is it this time really
got to be a record don't it
against logic and reason
i'm in the studio
four a.m. red bull
china shopping
married to
same old
acts

small poems for Big

twenty-four haiku for each year he lived

when you die, i'm told
they only use given names
christopher wallace

no notorious
neither b.i.g. nor smalls
just voletta's son

brooklyn resident
hustler for loose change, loosies
and a lil loose kim

let me tell you this
the west coast coast didn't get you
illest flow or nah

had our loyalties
no need to discuss that now
that your weight is dust

that your tongue is air
and your mother is coping
as only she can

i will also say
that i have seen bed stuy since
b.k. misses you

her walk has changed some
the rest of the borough flails
weak about itself

middle school students
not yet whispers in nine sev
know the lyrics rote

you: a manual
a mural, pressed rock, icon,
fightin word or curse

course of history
most often noted, quoted
deconstructed sung

hung by a bullet
prepped to die: *gunsmoke gunsmoke*
one hell of a hunch

here you lie a boy
twelve-gauge to your brain you can't
have what you want be

what you want you
black ugly heartthrob ever
conflicted emcee

respected lately
premier king of the casket
pauper of first life

til puff blew you up
gave you a champagne diet
plus cheese eggs, welches

you laid the blueprint
gave us word for word for naught
can't fault the hustle

knockoff messiah
slanged cracked commandments and saw
no honey, more problems

whole borough recoiled,
stillborn blacks, mourn genius slain
the ease of your laugh

the cut of your jib
unique command of the room
truthfully biggie

what about you's small
no not legend, not stature
real talk just lifespan

yo, who shot ya kid
nypd stopped searching
shrugged off negro death

well, we scour the sky
we mourn tough, recite harder
chant you live again

of all the lyrics
the realest premonition
rings true: you're dead. wrong

2pac couplets
one line for each year he lived

ninety six minutes after tyson wins and you're gone
las vegas quickly strips you of your last song

every black man in nevada pilgrims to trudge you
walk last rites, as only god can judge you

nomad, you baltimore, you new york, you l.a.
captured only by wind, a consummate stray

west coast makes you ours. claims you loudest
you gave game for free, we recoup it proudest

don't want no producers dancing in our videos
named our first borns after brenda's embryo

your dear mama, eschews her crackfiend fame
afeni becomes household, recognized name

the people used to clown when you came around
with the underground mimic and savior your sound

mark your ink, the lives of thugs on their stomachs
their bottoms, their rolling twenties, their hunneds

your words so sacrament so memorized so litmus
test and testament so wretched so generous

never knew malcolm as machiavellian text, hence
you vexed and cursing: our black and shining prince

our sweetest thing, our prism and its light
lynched by bullet, won't survive the knight

now your blood spills and the people crowd around
just one question:

r u
still
down?

ratchet

noun.
2. a situation or process that is perceived to be
deteriorating or changing steadily in a series
of irreversible steps.

gone and say something now
since you find yourself in lisa nails number three
in hawthorne or compton on a saturday at nine a.m.

vickie who is called something different in viet
is pulling frayed plastic from a tray and gluing it
to the underside of your top eyelid

the smell of acrylic acetone and fried hair wafting
everywhere you go you are called out your name
and now they have called you tool

something that is made to tighten loosen or hold fast
sht grl gone and claim it witcha yaki pack and tiny
waist and your impossible breasts

shrug your shoulders when they essentialize you
if they talk shit while you riding the 88 down fig
you roll your mfking eyes like grandma said:

(if the girl has managed to stay alive
in the face of all the things designed to kill her
make her go all the way metallic shades of crazy
like her hair's too tight and the wic store is closed
the one person she's ever trusted is evading child

support no one's ever asked her to speak a full sentence
and if they did they'd hear a bard
a legit lute for a mouthpiece call her ratchet if you want
doesn't change anything bout her circumstance,
her dilapidated high school or her need to yell
at the top of her lungs, when all of LA county tells her
to hush the outfit, her choice of music, her gum pop
is the subtle compromise between silence and homicide)

don't you choose the death, now.
gone and say something.

elevators (me & you)

a woman, once joined to him as lace to leather
must spit her name away like teeth
rise when he say, practice falls,
stay down.   if he threat, she considers how much
heavy he has on her. after the lift and drag,
the grainy footage, their foul step and repeat.
she's no one. nobody
has called her janay since the draft.

(then she thought, you were good, true,
but when the league took your body, who claimed mine
do i deserve whatever happens? will you train me
a weapon, an arm drawn and released

remember: how my voice carries in close and boxed space
            a scream or a prayer here is only yours to recount)

on being the other woman

i had four dollars in quarters exactly that i'd been saving
for the time i'd get on saturday to do the wash. it was late
as shit on tuesday when he called and an hour and a half
in my car assuming

no cops, no traffic, no second thoughts.
time at his place was uneventful, that's all i'll say.
it was warm and familiar. i laughed on his stomach.
brushed my teeth before we lay down.

he was brown. that's all i'll say.
i pulled the covers off of my face in the morning,
drove home lamenting poor decisions like
spending my last dollars on toll and not the laundry

on gas money and not my traffic fines
i got stuck in early morning commute in richmond
next to the oil refinery. when my music stopped playing
all that was left was the careful hum:

a cracked timing belt plus the way my panties collided
into themselves, pulled on in a hurry, chafing, matching
the way i told myself one day one day he'll care.

i was late to work and felt guilty then, too.
had to make up my hours on saturday, which was good.
since i couldn't afford to wash, anyway. that was
late summer. this is late fall.

he and i have been through for months now.
weeks at least. his smell is still all in my sheets.

sometimes he come through here, still the smile
he wear for her on. extra swipes of deodorant,

the toothpaste he like, wearing the t-shirt I bought him.
i can't be mad.   what can I say?
he smell like him. which I like.

liked.

sometimes i confuse my loneliness for his affection.
he say he don't even care for the way I kiss. won't touch me
unless he's a little bit drunk or has told himself
I matter more, in this moment.

he brings her to bed, often. at least the thoughts of her.
which make him sweat. which turns me on.
which makes me cry. and he's good about drying tears.
which means the three of us are lying

here.
together.

even when it's just me.
his scent is tangled in bedclothes I meant to wash
months ago. weeks, at least.
it's going to take time to undo this.

i borrowed four dollars from the kids upstairs to clean
the sheets. slept fitfully the first night I couldn't smell him.
tossed so hard I snapped the bed frame —

it's the cleanest break yet.

first date with the engaged rapper

the best handholding I ever did was in utah
me. an african. a blizzard.
the contrast.
the patterns.

snow flurries. his sable cheeks.
then a black-and-white talkie.
we outfoxed cold in a movie theater.
clasped first at the break in our pinkies,

i venture the interdict of his knuckles,
hands joined backwards gathered in the warm,
soft folds of his denim. as our palms finally
meet we are resigned to alleluia.

your stare is an unbridled laugh and mine too
but we cannot speak. we try rhymes instead, redact lines,
settle on saying nothing, bob heads,
count breaks

who are we to know such gleeful, tiny betrayal,
what right do we have to touch, rich and outlawed,
who dares find blackness in the snow and call it beautiful

e

i met her once. she looked like a young chaka, her favorite
singer, with a wig and the ten-gallon cowboy hat. she
describes herself as a texan, knowing full well that she's a
martian or a sorcerer and some shit. she talks out the corner
of her mouth like everything she say is common knowledge
and a secret. like niggas prize her genius but call it her ass
which, we should also say is prodigy. it is almost as if they
must pay homage and genuflect to her. carry bolts of fabric
and colts of 45 in their carry-on luggage, just to lay at her feet.
the greatest rhymes of our generation are afterthoughts, things
thunk once she rose from the bed to tend to wanting child,
ideas thrown over her shoulder in passing, now hooks and
verses quoted by the youngest of us, she shrine and madonna,
record and backspin, muse who drew dre to the truf and
drug lonnie to the turf and i imagine jay got so turned out he
decided nothing could be as good as the small gods in her
pocket and he gave up on black pussy and got reparations
directly from the source thereafter. i don't know. pure
conjecture on my part. i wonder if she broke up with them
all, if they left messages on her voicemail that she played for
her cousin-sisters on thursday evenings after the circles. i hail
the queen, who uses no throne though others encourage me
to watch theirs, i remember that she is rarely at liberty to cry,
to sing off-key, to delight in her own lonely, to pull the covers
over her head and wait for that bo willie brown all clear. she
is not allowed to go crazy or def or blind or pregnant even.
and yet she manages. timely and ancient.

life is good.

before i peeled off the vow
left not a gotdamned thing
in that house of yours
save this chiffon dear john

i did put it on once more
stared down the door
told myself *if* you beat sun up
maybe we can talk

i watched a pale green sky clap dawn into queens
put on my boyfriend jeans

                      and
                        left.

i wasn't even pissed
til i walked the perimeter of our bed
paced a song out my mouth
caught wind on my tongue
licked a scent from the air: lazy twat
some other's pube hair caught
in my teeth, nasty. fuck. i hate you so
much.   right now.

        i hate you. so much. right now
        i hate you. so much. right now

Drake questions the deceased, Vegas.

then aubrey stands over where it actually happened,
circles as a sufi, or chevy, singing off-key, properly
in his feelings, which makes the apparition arrive
agitated, on time, as drake hoped. bare-chested,
bandana-ed, ready. a brief interview followed:

is your favorite thing to place yourself inside
your own chalked outline on the boulevard
check your size against the mark, let your eyes dart,
search the throngs for suge?

since you are a phantom now,
don't you want to escape death
row, go north, to canada, and like me,
sing of danger but never face it, hide your life
from enemies or explosions in your chest?

don't you thank the bullet for making you a ghost,
for extracting you from the public eye? did you live
after that? is that when your songs became true?
i know you. see you. repeat you

that friday night on loop, you ignoring jada's pages,
watching the ring, the craze, tyson's eyes, how you begged
to see seldon spurt like a bellagio fount, and couldn't believe
it was you that'd been hit

til a cop swaddled your head, asked *who did this*
who did this and all you knew to say, all that made sense
was *fuck.*

you. shoulda said more to the crusted desert of drunks,
slots of woke men who have loved you but never admitted
and never let go, if you had been taught fame
was a hate crime against black men,

would you have still stepped in the booth?
do you wish they would mourn you and let you die?
we *should* draw casino light to our eyes,
raise your blood in glasses, recite kaddish,

but we both know no one commits prayer
to melody. so now may i perform? your exorcism.
stand over your body, serene, search your smile for signs
of my own and we mouth together:

> *oh my god*
> *oh my god*
> *if i die*
> *i'm a legend*
>
> *oh my god*
> *oh my god*
> *if i die i'm a legend*

Mr. Carter watches *The Godfather* on the day his daughter is to be married.

like twelve and a half minutes in, shawn takes his feet
off of the desk to laugh.

no no no pause the shit for a second pause the shit
grant a meeting to all these neutral until they need me
friends? if you believe in america. and are raised on america
and still believe in that shit before you believe in me and
you come to my beautiful baby girl's first and only wedding day
to ask me a favor. i gotta grant you a meeting?

fuckouttahere.

all i ever done is listen to streets, all i pushed for, this day,
no let me finish
one moment alone when I might call me my given name and
raise my child, like an over-runneth cup, to the heavens,
have baby see her own color as a triumph, call her blue,
knowing moving white what financed her joy,
alongside an unspoken trail of crimson,
all the bodies that had to vanish in order to cement
her happiness, this america and here i am both god,
the father and

you could press play again

the ballad of Hollywood

Court, my brother, per judge order, sports
a crisp button-up to anger management
at browns mill rec every other friday and
since the money spent figures shit
he oughta get an evening out, too.

hollywood turn left in the hallway mirror,
then three-quarters, pudges out his gut,
retracts it, inspects shirt warp and weft,
his collar bends, he smooths the silk,
looks the kind of good black men only
dream of being.

when he mimics grandpop's smile,
spooks himself. see no teeth. sees
a cobweb overtaking a spider, imagines
himself a trap and prey nothing new to speak

must be the old english, his lips surround
glass as if it is a suspect, he knocks back
the corner of malt liquor and hits the club
a spot where you go to get your lil first taste

a nightlife where *everything* goes wrong
dj keep wheeling up set it off

someone spills drank down the right
arm, or the left, maybe.
it all blends together
let the liquor tell it

Court see the stain before he feel it,
liquor spreads across the shirt like a
surface wound
all *damn*
           damn damn
                        damn from here

he revels in a burst of heat
screams *i just got this mufuckin shirt*
pushes his angry into a mouth
clears it of porcelain
the soft gush of flesh
the quickening heart
dew bursting across pores

he can't hold it now. he tried.
he is nets and arachnid now
eight arms into a body, the body,
the body, of some *other* lil nigga
sinks his cagey bite, a knife to a neck

and for an instant, he levitates
           he the master and the servant
           the preacher, the congregation
           the pussy, the come here finger
           the swirling lights, an angel's chorus,

you got to understand, he knows it's fleeting
but when he draws someone's blood away
from its course and holds it in his mouth
and fist at once he tastes tomorrow.

he does feel like a new man
thumps a fist against his heart

invincible.
invincible. invincible!
he cry, or maybe ellison royale,
may be invisible?

and just like that he back in his atlanta club.
broke in a rich black man's town
returned to earth with the cops arriving

he tears down his chest.
pops buttons, shirt off

he gasp hard
gasp hard again
now
he sob he say
now

who else wanna fuck
who else wanna fuck with
Hollywood Court?

lose your self

about illinois more than it is about michigan
about kankakee corn more than eight mile
about lighting things afire, watching them dance the dark out
about smoking hot whiteness centered in my black mother's eyes

if she had been born later paler more west
my mother would be marshall mathers
she would pick meat from rappers' bones for sport
like she does now. the way em has always done
keep it one hunned my mom has always liked
country & western, fancied sad ballads
about unremarkable towns &
she has painstakingly coffined secrets
in maize fields behind her own mother's house
once she lost herself on the short drive between
her room on southbrook and the ice cream parlor
where she shoveled electric blue dessert:
cold product for klansmen
knew she was the biggest thing in kankakee,
the brightest, most often choked light my mother
has always been
         a genius
             at the end
                  of a rope
a disaster waiting to happen in the grocery
she would not
grow old in salem's lot
so when we first saw the movie
& she watched her black quiet
fortysomething-year-old self
lodged inside the body of a young, white boy
pasted back inside a black culture nothing

but unabashedly himself i won't lie to you
and say she cried my momma ain't never cried
about no rap song, but if you were there, like me,
you would have seen her dimmest bulb brighten,
she quoting lyrics all through holiday dinner
preparation, pacing the house repeating
her favorite bit

                               mom's spaghetti
ha   *mom's spaghetti*
she boils the noodles
steam plays in her silver hair
knife shakes in her hands
her palms are sweaty

about illinois as much as crazy hospitals
about kankakee as much as missing grandma
about time as much as losing it
about minds as much as losing it

Jordan Davis'
broken ghazal *(after Aaron Samuels)*

with best friends at nothing gas station
got sound turned up so loud can't help but feel you

when the system yanks the bass of your neck it's closest
you ever feel to god every other instant you're hunted you

haunted wanted vaunted attacked so black
dark   alone   gone head you

love the crew live for the weeknd   party next door
die by friday   you

cry *mercy*   so thirsty cashed in iced tea, hoodies,
fun-sized candies, new years, bachelor parties. you

have hidden everywhere one can hide a black body
you have gone there clung to bars unsafe how you

petrol stop threat when he's who fired nine then left
just boys   shot up   in time you

fall away   he say he standing his ground well
so are we —   he's gone now and so also you

here steel gasps rattled bumpers flashing lights
too late ambulance & this is what it means to be you

seventeen with a life wish wanting a song stuck
in your head   & instead   getting a bullet.

the Oscars
(an epic for Ryan Coogler)

1.
I have this brother who is a dragon.
He dances best under crescent moons.
Drinks sulfur for breakfast.
Breathes it out of his nose.

He became a creature at age ten.
When Jordan, a ginger kid at Redwood Heights
Summer Program called my fire-
eating brother the nword in front
of his crush, well —

he grew eight feet tall and stomped
the old country out the boy
then bashed his head on the concrete
til a playground monitor
pulled him off.

He's got some anger issues.

You should check the hoop court there.

You should look.

There is still blood.

2.
I have a brother who is a unicorn
so tall you have to crane your neck to meet him.
His thoughts are ivory that protrude from the center
of his head, make him awkward in mixed company.

He carries his genius as a horn.
The tallest black kid on Stanford's campus.
The white engulfs him like a tee shirt copped at a liquor store
creased and edging for his knees.

He doesn't cry. Ever. Unicorns can't cry
in open meadows. In their dorm rooms. In the dark.
They are held down. Struggle against it.

My brother knows. He knows.
There are men made to hunt him, to buzz
saw his thoughts off, make him a regular stallion.
A race horse. Change his name and make him glue.

He's a neuroscientist who likes Keak.

He calculates.

He knows to be quiet.

He keeps to himself, thinking all of the time.

3.
Got this bruh who is an octopus.
He has eight arms and plays the drums.
Tours the world selling Europeans safe rap.
He is the only black man in his group.

They play France. They play Germany.
They play Covington, Kentucky.
He rocks with his shirt off.
The white boys crowd the stage.

He likes to drink a good lager.
He never cheats on his girlfriend.

He is not sure he believes in God.
He knows how to talk to an officer.

He is good with authority.

Ask anyone, he is really, really good with authority.

Thinks most cops are fine people.

Thinks he'll live forever, like most octopi do.

4.
My play brother is a house fly trapped in a cake dish.
Everytime he hits the wall of his cell a wing falls off.
He is serving two consecutive forty-two-year terms at Folsom
State Prison. I put money on his books at the Walgreens
across from City Hall. He trusts me. They won't let me
come visit. He calls me his woman. I'm not.
He tells me the food there is shit.
He wants to eat my cooking under a sunrise.
He been gone nine years.

Hasn't seen any parts of dawn since he was a boy.
He killed someone, accidentally, and could die hovering
over corn mush, wingless, under heavy surveillance
in a farm town just off the Five. Not too far from Bakersfield.

He got a contraband phone, maybe.

Maybe I was passing the prison and texting him

and you when the Zimmerman verdict hit.

Maybe y'all said the same exact thing.

The same thing exactly.

5.
My lover is the safest black man in American television.
Paid to be. South Dakota welcomes him into their homes
once a week. He isn't allowed to yell in public.
He has been weaned off opinions this charged unless
he says em over a beat. He is playing draughts with sweeps,
his finger on a king. He wants to jump everybody.
Stressed out about his sister who can't find an apartment and
his brother who is sometimes left alone and his mother
who worries about her boys so far away and his dad.
His dad too.

My lover's a broken safety on a four-five.

He and any gun will shoot if triggered.

They ask him to sing to make records.

If a needle drops it'll be like a pin from a grenade.

When they said it was fine for the boy to lay there
and the killer to walk. I was just outside of Folsom, drove
straight to his house. Waited for him to get off set.
He held me while I sobbed.

He said 'fuck' all night long. Then 'Jesus.'
Then put his tears in my uncombed hair.

6.
There is a single black man I want to die.
He is unremarkable.

He keeps on testing me.

He keeps on testing me.

There is a single black man I want to die.

7.
The first boy I ever kissed with my tongue is a canary
covered in coal. He thought for a time he could not fly up
only down into dangerous places where diamonds aren't
found. He quit his mining job and took a long hot shower.

Stood in front the mirror, puffed out his pecs,
looking at his body all gold and shit, while Trinidad James
played from a phone speaker. My first kiss is getting his life
in order. And is nothing like the day they arrested him. He
is sleek, soft to touch, a black buffed so tough he starts to
shine. His smile is fake but that is a different story,
one where someone took a bat to his face and wiped the
chalk out the blackboard of his mouth. Real talk.
All my goons been through it.

Everyone black man I love been through it.

This one the most, maybe.

This one life keep coming at like an electric train.

Like a bad night at the start of the year.

He ain't got no kids yet.

8.
and then there's you.
where to begin.

pretty sure you're a gryphon.
a lion with a shorn mane.
an eagle with a growl like a beast of prey.
you fly into a room. everybody goes silent.

you hate that part.
i know.

you see yourself down on that platform.
you see your own mama wailing over you.

you see yourself a bloody dog
pressed to a black boy's chest

and paraded down 7th street
you still can't watch the end of your movie

you know what it does
you know what it does

9.
the theater at Grand Lake, your favorite cinema
is packed, all night, with men, with low cuts,
skeptical eyes, with grudges and trust issues,
with pamphlets, with offspring, with mothers, free
popcorn, final calls, peach optimos, twenty-dollar eighth
specials, one

is your brother. the other one Noah too, your mother,
your father, my father with whom you almost shared
a birthday, the people who are unsure you're the right one
to tell this story, everyone who couldn't get into the Weinstein
screenings, my unicorn is there, my coal-stained canary there,
my housefly is still away, the safe one won't see it for months,
my octopus is out entertaining, the dragon is still too angry,

my next door neighbor, who lost his best friend in Miami,
high school boys, group home kids, the starting five on
Mack's team, the Eastlake band, men who kept growing
locks, even after you cut yours, the one black man I want
dead, the kids he mentors, my stepfather, all came, in a single-
file line, to sing this dirge with you, to see if a demon could
be released, to test if they were still magic as they thought,
even if they lost a wing, changed color, had their best horns
chopped off, or cried in my unruly mane.

my brother the unicorn sobbed
in front of the theater.
in the company of all these men.
left snot on my father's shoulder.

my dad called a week later to tell me
he wasn't doing very well.
we saw him shaken.
it was hard for him, but good.

I was there.

You were not.

I am supposed to tell you.

They are all Oscars.

10.
they are golden, solemn men, who stand frozen,
cup hands to their chests, wait to be prized.
say you cannot put them on any mantle.
they are not academy sanctioned.

there will not, tonight, or any other day
be red carpets rolled ahead of them.
no coverage of the moment.
no film, even, when they are killed.

but every one of them is yours.
every figure they have become
a monument to ache you must feel
in the cutting room, lucas, at cannes,

park city, everywhere you have gone,
alone, braving this anger, answering
with metered, appropriate responses
you have taken each of these statues

home

they are with you.

each of them

with you.

the corner.

so the real niggas call javon soft.
he should have been at least still
at golden hour if not moving weight.
but von wanted to read.

when he asked me to show him how
was the only time i ever saw his bad tooth,
no smiling or wincing with this one. strong.
he waited on my stoop curled into *honey,*

i love. i like Greenfield. he marveled at my index
finger. which touched the pages but drew no sound
from his mouth. i'd point at a word. wait. make him
put the sound together. eventually.

Eloise seeped slowly out from under his loose
bicuspid. magic, he say.

i ask him why — no — *what* he scared to love.
he say *a lot of things,*
a whole lot of things.

he wakes early, makes alarm of car door
drags rubber across cement
sneakers: shoes and wearer
he drowns out birds' morning song
with hot cheetos in queso in tin-lined bags
lips stained brown after too many blacks
and pall malls. here, if you are a man you must

stand here. post at store, speak hello to statues
roll west around your mouth
lick despair off as candy as shells
decorate chocolate men.

if you are weak, they say, *do not stand with us.*
if you leave you must be against us and so
javon never learned.

never told nobody that. and i never will.

i refuse to snitch the block's secrets
remember this crook of the town best
of all the hamlets i've chosen to be
or not to be.

i recall his important stories

retain the rough and unseemly,

put that on cithas

spin it in circles

like a doughnut

like a sideshow

like a treasured 45

light privilege or Lili speaks
for mo browne

2.
if say for example we are in the liquor store
on adeline and hollis and a actual real life black girl
tell you your hair look like it got some white
in it, you take it as the compliment she intends

pretend you don't know the accusation
make her feel it is her idea don't you know
if you beautiful you supposed to deny it
you not supposed to let on you considered
how so much finer you are than her

3.
oh yeah & whitley gilbert & freddie
& denise the pretty one & sandra
the second prettiest & rudy had long hair
but don't make the cut & raven symone
& winnie & nelson & justine justine & claire
of course & absolutely not

not cousin pam & not vanessa of course
& not vanessa of course & not if she end
up with dabnis & they'll have the darkest
huxtables and he work in sanitation too
please

4.
to be born this light
is to direct traffic from the center

of an isosceles triangle
etched over the atlantic

take caribbean sugar
take all the spice in india
i'll be the milk in your light
skin caffeine rush

i'm what moved the industrial revolution
live from the factories in london

redbones have gathered the whole world's
sorrow in a teaspoon and their shade
in the palm of a hand

5.
and of course the first light baby in the new world
was the first admission of the enslaved's defeat

6.
oh my god what are you mixed with
oh my god what are you mixed with
oh my god what are you mixed with

you don't even know
if i had hair like yours
i would _____

7.
i can go swimming if i want to
i can dance harder at the club
i can ask the boys to prom
i can sleep no rag sleep no track
sex no worry gym no issue

i get in the deep end i can go
swimming if i want to

8.
from five hundred feet away
a white woman sees us roll up

our sleeves put forearms next to each other
from this distance an act of sorority

but up close
a ranking it is
hands free paper
bag device

9.
and in the bank oh my god what are you mixed with
and in the grocery oh my god what are you mixed with
and in church don't speak as much
let the dark girl get the solo

10.
good & bad hair see
if i care. good &
bad
hair
wanna be better than me

11.
oh my god what are you mixed with
oh my god what are you mixed with
oh my god what are you mixed with

got to be something you don't get
hair like that behaving black

12.
and how i apologize for a million hurtful acts
i can say i never did or never knew as pain
like taking shayla thompson by the hand
parading her around the school yard
take her chin see profile right
center profile left fingernails
grade of hair

ask all of the boys marcus turner
john sharper justin pleasants
which one of us the most beautiful
no duh

13.
see?
dark girl tears keep my hair straight

14.
sth
pft
sith
pft
ha
they
aint
never
going
to make
no princess
tiana your
color.

15.
& you can feel it
in the one drop

16.
how many times you think they asked barry
if he was sure, if he wanted a pretty girl or michelle

17.
my best friend's best friend meleia before
they shot her had a theory about mixed girls
with black mommas and mixed girls with white mommas and
how the first ones is black
and the second ones is white and it's about
how you learn
what to ask for
in the world

she say she always been glad
her momma so black

18.
sula x huck finn
beloved x atticus finch
spike x tarantino

19.
vanessa williams the first to do it
heavy lies the crown

halle berry the first to do it
heavy lies the crown

miss america goes to the monster's ball

20.
what color are your eyes
what color are your eyes
what color would you say your eyes are

hazel

gray maybe

1.
let's be honest jet stream
let's be real tire mark
keep it one hunned field mob

i think that i'm cute
because i am because i am
better than you i think
that i am cute because i am
i think that i'm better because
the whole world believes it to be true

and ain't that the truth
and ain't that the truth

crude portraits of the Lower Bottoms

*

these ngas
seen me for years
i've watched their hair gray
and stature change

as if this here corner store
is god marking the passing of time and height
like flowered wallpaper
etched in graphite

this tall nineteen eighty-eight
this tall two thousand and thirteen
these men still push their backs to the wall
as if to keep the institution from crumbling

these ngas in front the store
popping yang like always
turn soft metal atop forty ounces expertly

these black men shaped like wrought iron spires
who still call each other out like
nga why you let yourself lose
that job and why you keep hollering
at ancient girls and how long will we stand
out in the cold anyway

and they look up the block at approaching cars
and decide to stay here just a few minutes longer

**

sarah tramble and her house full of clothing
and her books full of clippings
and the late-model car left under a tan tarp
and the garden she tends in the right time

the herbs she is keeping in a white cloth
the parchment she has been saving for decades
the dress forms she has always used
her hatred for the miniskirt she saw in

1923, 1974, two thousand and whatever
honey, she seen em, don't like em.

sarah tramble and her tongue like barb
her wit like wire her body like locomotive in forward motion

to be ninety-nine
of louisiana
but been here long enough to have taught school
been a nurse. married and remarried after one left
for one reason or another or death or another

sarah tramble has seen the neighborhood turn itself
over and over and now, she is in her front room,
watching the same hustles and new u-hauls

* * *

beauty supply warehouse
on the corner of west grand and market
with every sort of fake attachment
one can put into her hair
every shade of lipstick
one can trace onto her lips
every style of gel or matte or gloss for nails
the girls come here
get pretty
to themselves
they get pretty
to themselves
they look like flowers,
pressed between pages,
then laminated

sure, gorgeous,
sure, easy to move

but what about the live rose with thorns
what about the dangerous beauties,
americans never picked?

the b side.

we were drunk off survival at the white bar
your brothers hollering at thickies in rainbow dresses
you got me for a song, bought me liquor after
liquor i couldn't afford.
reminded we'd both be thirty, come fall
you wanted me. with your father's squint asked twice
to have your children. you did that. in oakland.

> i am *nothing*
> like how you make me
> in the verses, you know
>
> this void i plead be spackled over
> with a black child who can't leave and
> for decades i've thought myself too ugly
> damaged and smart to deserve anyone
>
> i *told* you i worry all my lovers recast me with
> prettier, easier, origami versions of me.
> like you did in the video, remember.
> tell the truth

you took me stumbling dumb ecstatic to a grand white
hotel at the edge and top of my town
bit the fleshy gap between my knuckles
played me til naked with frankie beverly and the jones girls
so when the rubber slipped and you just kept on, well,
i imagined you was for real.

the morning after. you wanted it gone. even the idea.
you left the engine running didn't even think to pay
at walgreens on fifty-first. i overdrew my account. said ah
and waved my tongue. swallowed the pill. this is what is done.

i held my crotch and vomited in secret that day
while we drove your brothers sightseeing. in oakland.

no childhood
(after Kim Addonizio)

lonely drank came in paper cups no umbrellas
the twenties a decade of wakes
every body craved a black
each casket begged a bouquet

our twenties a decade of wakes
no one could open their eyes
each casket begged a bouquet
we learned to roll one handed

lee wouldn't open his eyes
lay there like the dead friends
and we learned to roll short handed
take shots and pull hard

play dead with our live friends
split brown spines cast away the excess
pull hard and take shots
blunts and stupor our only luxuries

our split brown spines cast away as excess
everybody craved a black
those stupid blunts our only luxury
the drank came in solo cups no fucking umbrellas

sunset

1.
i don't mind if we use the tip of your tongue
to push thoughts back into my mouth

i don't even mind if you hush my whispers
let it be unspoken:

the surprising calm of watching los angeles
dawn over your rising and falling chest

this unmistakable longing your bed
your brow your index finger still have

for her. always the her. though she is gone
and i am here, with a handful of sweet everything

i don't mind if we don't talk about it if we rush
into each other as well water does to thirsty

deserts as teenagers do to supple bodies
as long as you are here and i am here and

smog runs rings around the skyline
let that be our metaphor

the dirty, the unused, the unwanted commonplace
that make the usual sky nine arresting shades of pink at dusk.

2.
(look at that. just like that. i have dreamed all day of you.
i imagine you in the pale light of morning
the harried thick of lunch and coffee and cigarette
breaks. you break. so consistently you break the

husk off of me. look at you singing on a sunday
craving church specially since you don't pray anymore

i don't worship you. not my style. my faith is wider
but here, in the chill amber of a day when we woke
wrapped inside each other. and for lots of reasons
i hurried out of your bed and into the day

only to say
i am never ready to leave you.

and then we suck the brittle off of each other's lips
as a way of not actually uttering goodbye

and just like that the day has passed
and i want you by night, too)

sex on a tour bus

or really the next day when i am in the wash and we are snaking through western mass on the ride to fenway or house of blues. i consider the designers. praise them. who deemed it necessary for a full bed, a functional toilet, an operable shower and even night stands. who thought to construct this in the loins of an multi-passenger auto, where up front your bassist is riding sawed-off shotty and giving madden twenty fourteen the bidness, where along the belly of the coach sleep your brothers, their two threes and jordans in neat rows under the lowest bunks. i wonder if they heard us last night? when we made a wide turn to keep the bus on the right route, and you had to anchor by pinning your wrist to the small of my back, oh, when someone else was responsible for the curves and movement and all i had to do was ride? blessings on the architects and even the road that smuggles you away nine months of the year.

really, i want to talk about the next morning when we are parked and still you tell me to go ahead and use the last hot water and wash my hair for real and i call myself a groupie and this is the only thing that makes you angry and, you remind, that's impossible because your brothers love me. we are a thin pane discussion, me writing your name backwards in the fog so you can notice how carefully i practice marking the signs of you.

this is when i realized it is *always* going to be us. me titties uneven and fatter than the girls in the front row and you ravenous for me anyway. how i finally call you into the shower and we dance there with no water and no time and no space between.

vows

there is a place in you i can tell what needs
healing: a something you keep wrapped in blue
wool and cotton balls and old sunday funnies
tucked up near corrugated boxes marked "not to
be touched" / i locate you amidst the wreckage,
boxes of kleenex, live and fired grenades, roses
wilted and fresh, too / you got that one upbeat
mike number that breaks you down to yellow tears
in your beat-up denim on your mama's parquet /
your right knee keeps trouble from sideways leaning
when you dance / you are no stranger to pain.
i am drawn to these places, again.
again.
again.

so many reasons to protect yourself. for one, they will always
leave, your men, half a mug of tea as their goodbye. you like
me are troubled mostly by the way the light just sank out of
your first love's eyes — a friday at sunset and it was over. after
all this time you are alone.
again.
again.

so, i can oath you just this. i have left
and then i have been left. i will not abandon you,
simply will not stomach the idea, must attend to
these gorgeous or unscathed pieces or cragged
homely awful bits, my stars! hand to my mouth, i do
believe

you want to be touched, as only i can imagine it, i think
all of this ache you felt was just you stumbling toward me
and all the joy you knew becomes so pale by our light and
if you should ever forget that, it too will be a place what needs
mending, and i will tell you again.
again.
again.

bouncing back
(or the woman listens to Prince
while writing Mystikal in prison).

I keep combing you out of my hair. For real, standing in the
mirror, naked as the day my mother made me, dripping wet
from my shower, eyeing the left nipple, which skews right
and the breast that is slightly larger than its counterpart. I
have been waxed nearly bald everywhere but my head and I
am slipping a rat-tailed comb into my mane at sixty-degree
angles. Separating into neat sections.

Aha. There you are, falling across my forehead as true glitter,
one thousand pieces of glass I'm trying to pluck from my face.
Before my eyes start to watering. Before this bathroom debris
gets the best of me.

It has been a week since I closed the door behind you and
told you to go. You knocked again, once, a very gentle knock
of apology, and I had half a mind to let you back in and fuck
you once more just to prove I still could. Digusting. I've been
vomiting in small doses. A teaspoon-and-a-half of refuse at a
time. In my mouth, on my toothbrush, against the heel of my
hand. I've been scrubbing the backs of my knees, the rough
parts of my feet, the webbing between my digits, the thick
flab flap between my arms and chest, the elastic bits of my
earlobe, the waxy dirt in my navel.

I've performed an enema, taken every expectorant there is,
hopped up on vicodin, spitting up yellow phlegm and rub-
bing my fingerpads over the rosary of my knuckles. Hail Mary.
I'm throwing my arms up and calling in sick.

There's no day off for this. I tell them I have a cold. And it's going to last two weeks, at least. I might lose the gig, but if I go in, and have to explain that I let you hold me down, that you told me to take it, that my best friend was in the next room and at twenty-five I wasn't brave enough to kill you dead with the lamp on my nightstand, with the nightstand, with the dark patch of night itself – if I have to go in and make nice and not tell another story of a black girl getting robbed for her body in her own home by a man with whom she thought she had a compact, a stitch of trust – I will willingly loose my mind to the ether. I will turn my thoughts to moths and free them one at a time into a shoe box. I'll shake the cardboard and rattle the flightless flying things 'til their wings fall off. And then eat them to know their taste and wonder why they don't have bones.

I'm going crazy.

I don't want to call the police. I've performed my own kit. I've swabbed good and hard, with the cleanest washcloth I could find. Ain't that enough? And all that's there is the licorice root and peppermint odor you slide across your scalp.

I'll keep examining my body for signs of you. But all that's there is this Prince song that was playing when it happened. And now every time I comb my hair, thoughts of you get in my eyes.

for my best friend in the year of his marriage

my laughs with you live on the edge of a puddle
and at the end of that puddle a beam of light

we are eastern parkway after the parade
where it rains every year

the storm strokes slow across the shoulders

men groping for enough lung power to be heard
against the sound of speakers on trucks

i fancy you like that
a yell transferred as whisper

scarcely heard sopping wet irresponsible
giggly hard asking nothing but time

we are fiercely candid about everything
except this one thing

that grew out of comfort
tangled into otherwise casual talk

bullies us only when we are near enough
to acknowledge our laughter

is the one thing that'll break it
so I place it next to water and sun

in a fantasy where good things grow

notes for Smoke before he meets my father

a.
baba has always kept a garden behind our house
when he first turned the soil, he took machetes
to errant bamboo.

the more he chopped, the more adamant it became
as if, true to word, it were a metal
did you know it is a grass

did you know it will keep on coming back
whether or not you notice it
or want it to, it will resurface wherever it is planted

dad fought it tooth and nail
and one day it fell away.

b.
we had a fire in the house
everything curled into damage

including the floorboards in the kitchen
excluding the garden behind the house

when insurance came through
and dad got to replace the linoleum and carpet

he opted for bamboo
old foe turned new standard

like a poe thump in reverse
our grass undid all the tell-tale signs of death

c.

if my heart is bamboo

if these single lines find nothing to partner them

if there are no couplets left in the matching

if my heart is a weed being excised from a garden

cut it down to the root

chop it hard and fast

make a stump of it.

flatten it right quick smooth

and make it lumber

towards the place you put your feet

when you are hungry

d.
if my heart is bamboo
grass that will not quit

and i am meant to be two
with you: come find me behind my father's house

a wild machete in hand, bending back grass
we will repurpose in due time.